British Library Cataloguing in Publication Data

A catalogue record for this book is
available from the British Library

ISBN 0340 87900 9

First published in hardback in 2003
This paperback edition published 2004

Published by Hodder Children's Books,
a division of Hodder Headline Limited,
338 Euston Road, London NW1 3BH

10 9 8 7 6 5 4 3 2 1

Originated by Dot Gradations Ltd, UK

Printed in China

PLOO AND THE TERRIBLE GNOBBLER

MICK INKPEN

Hodder
Children's
Books

A division of Hodder Headline Limited

The story starts like this. There is a dog with a blue nose tugging at the bedclothes. His name is Dig. Suddenly, from under the bedclothes, another blue nose. It belongs to Ploo.

Outside the window, in a bokonut tree, a Little Honk Owl is honking gently at the stars, through its blue beak. It is a new day on Blue Nose Island. Or at least it should be. But why is the Little Honk Owl still honking? Why is it still dark?

And why are there bokonuts all over the floor?

Ploo gets up and goes to the window. Down below, his best friend, Hatz, is about to throw another bokonut.

'At last! You're awake!' says Hatz.

'Come quickly! Something terrible has happened!' And then, all in one breath, 'There are no oggs! No oggs for breakfast! The bouncy hens aren't bouncing, so there are no oggs!

They won't wake up!

Because it's still dark!

Because the sun hasn't come up!

Because the moon is stuck! LOOK!'

He is pointing at Blue Nose Volcano.

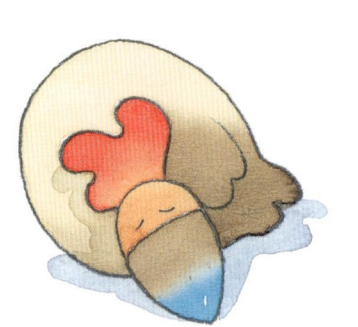

It is true. The moon has hooked itself in a bokonut tree at the top of Blue Nose Volcano. Down on the beach everyone is talking about it.

Ploo says that someone will have to climb the bokonut tree and unhook the moon. Everyone agrees.

There is a long silence. Everyone is thinking of the Gnobbler, the Terrible Gnobbler that lives at the top of Blue Nose Volcano.

After a while Ploo says that he will have to climb the bokonut tree as he is the smallest and lightest, apart from Bo who is too young.

Everyone breathes a sigh of relief.

'I'll come too,' says Hatz.

Before long he has reached the lagoon at the
foot of Blue Nose Volcano.

B ut Ploo slips away with Dig on his own.
Hatz, he thinks, will make too much noise
and wake the Gnobbler.

Before long he has reached the lagoon at the
foot of Blue Nose Volcano.

'Stay away from the edge!' he says to Dig.
Why does he say that do you think? Because the
lagoon is full, not of water, but of sky and clouds.
It is no place to throw a stick for a dog to fetch.
If you dive in you will not sink, oh no.
You will fall for ever and ever.

Ploo stops to look for a while, then
heads off into the junglywood that
grows up the slopes of Blue Nose.

A lagoony watches him go.

The junglywood is Ploo's favourite place.
It is full of the sound of jingletrees and
bellvine. And everywhere are noths and
butterflutters, hecklers and babberchats,
slithery snooks, bandicoots and tiddlerfrogs.

But today, or is it tonight, there's no time
to stop and look. For as they climb higher,
Dig stops suddenly and listens.

There is another sound.
A grumbling, rumbling roar. A terrible snore.

The Gnobbler is asleep.

Good.

On top of Blue Nose, the Gnobbler's snores rise up like thunder.
Carefully Ploo slips off Dig's lead and tells him to stay. Then he tiptoes, quiet as a diddymouse, around the crater rim towards the bokonut tree, freezing like a statue in the silences between the snores.

He grips Dig's lead between his teeth and begins to climb. Soon his arms ache and his feet begin to slip. And as he climbs high, the bokonut tree begins to bend. It bends towards the big black hole and the sound of thunder.

Hold on, Ploo! Hold on!

And don't look down!

T he bokonut bounces,

once,

twice,

three times on the crater rim

and down into the black hole.

Plop!

The snoring stops.

Keep quiet, Ploo! And hold on!

He is at the top.

He can barely hold on.

But he takes Dig's lead and swings it through the air. Swish. Swish. He flicks it at the pointy end of the crescent moon.

It misses.

Try again, Ploo. Swish. Swish.

Yes! The lead has hooked the moon!

Gently now. Gently. He tugs the lead.

The moon tilts.

The tree groans.

A bokonut begins to fall . . .

But Ploo cannot hold on any longer.
  He falls too. He grabs at the lead, which
tugs the moon and sends it spinning like a great,
silent catherine wheel up into the night sky.

The bokonut tree unbends and shakes off the
rest of its bokonuts. Ploo falls, head over tail,
turning and catching a glimpse, for the first time,
inside Blue Nose. There is nothing but blackness
and a terrible roaring in his ears.

P loo bounces on Blue Nose.
He spins like a little rag doll
right over Dig and tumbles down into
the junglywood.

And what with the rolling and the tumbling
and the spinning in his head, and the bouncing of
the bokonuts all around, and the screeching of the
babberchats, and Dig's barking, he cannot tell
whether the Terrible Gnobbler is right behind
him snapping at his heels, or not.

And it doesn't much
matter anyway . . .

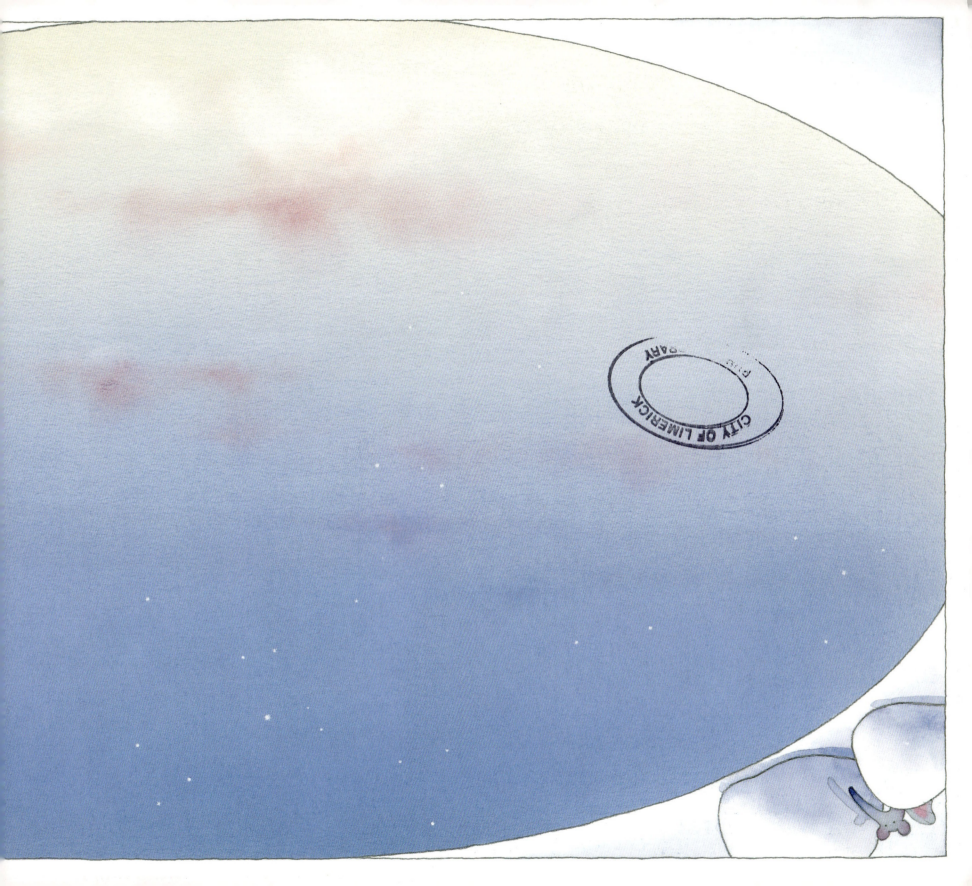

. . . because he tumbles
straight into Blue Nose Lagoon.
And suddenly all is quiet except
for the sound of Dig barking.

Another sound. Swish. Creak. Swish. Creak.
The sound of Ploo swinging backwards and
forwards on the end of Dig's lead. He is dangling
above sky and clouds and nothing much else.

And as he dangles there, we'll let him catch
his breath, and watch as the sun begins to rise
at last over Blue Nose Island . . .

. . . which is no ordinary island, as you can see.

It is morning at last. The Little Honk Owl flies home to roost in the junglywood and the bouncy hens begin to bounce.

Breakfast is late on Blue Nose Island, and later still for Ploo who takes a while to haul himself out of the lagoon and walk back home. He is a hero, of course. Everyone says so.